PENGUIN LIFE

HOW TO LET THINGS GO

Shunmyo Masuno, the head priest of a 450-year-old Zen Buddhist temple in Japan, is the author of the international bestsellers *Don't Worry* and *The Art of Simple Living* as well as an award-winning Zen garden designer for clients around the world. He is a professor of environmental design at one of Japan's leading art schools and has lectured widely, including at the Harvard Graduate School of Design, Cornell University, and Brown University.

ALSO BY SHUNMYO MASUNO

The Art of Simple Living

Don't Worry

HOW TO LET THINGS GO

99 Tips from a Zen Buddhist Monk
to Relinquish Control and
Free Yourself Up for What Matters

SHUNMYO MASUNO

Translated by Allison Markin Powell

life

PENGUIN BOOKS
An imprint of Penguin Random House LLC
penguinrandomhouse.com

Copyright © 2021 by Shunmyo Masuno

Translation copyright © 2024 by Allison Markin Powell

A Penguin Life Book

Originally published in Japanese as *Houtte oku chikara*
by Mikasa-Shobo Publishers Co., Ltd., Tokyo.

This English-language edition is published by arrangement with Mikasa-Shobo Publishers Co., Ltd., Tokyo, c/o Tuttle-Mori Agency, Inc., Tokyo.

LIBRARY OF CONGRESS CATALOGING-IN-PUBLICATION DATA
Names: Masuno, Shunmyō, author.
Title: How to let things go : 99 tips from a Zen Buddhist monk to relinquish control and free yourself up for what matters / Shunmyo Masuno ; translated by Allison Markin Powell.
Other titles: Shigoto mo ningen kankei mo umaku iku hōtteoku chikara. English
Description: New York : Penguin Life, [2024]
Identifiers: LCCN 2024015282 (print) | LCCN 2024015283 (ebook) | ISBN 9780143138136 (hardcover) | ISBN 9780593512272 (ebook)
Subjects: LCSH: Spiritual life—Zen Buddhism. | Worry—Religious aspects—Buddhism. | Conduct of life.
Classification: LCC BQ9288 .M36313 2024 (print) | LCC BQ9288 (ebook) | DDC 294.3/44—dc23/eng/20240706
LC record available at https://lccn.loc.gov/2024015282
LC ebook record available at https://lccn.loc.gov/2024015283

Printed in the United States of America
1st Printing

Set in Berling LT with Opal LT
Designed by Sabrina Bowers

CONTENTS

PART ONE

Don't get overly involved.

Be more detached in your relationships.

PART TWO

Don't worry about every little thing.

How to relinquish anxiety, impatience, and anger

PART THREE

Be measured in your reactions.

Practices that won't wear down your spirit

PART FOUR

Don't waste your energy.

Ways to avoid making things more difficult for yourself

PART FIVE

Don't see everything as black or white.

Hints for living a comfortable life

FOREWORD

Those who have the power to let
things go are not at the mercy of
their personal relationships.

They don't feel compelled to be constantly connected on
social media, so they don't monitor their friends by text
24/7, nor do they get caught up in gossip.

They know that friendship is about quality over quantity. They're good at disregarding the opinions and actions
of people they don't even know.

Those who have the power to let
things go are able to eliminate
distractions at work.

They aren't easily swayed by others, so they don't obsess
over the judgments of their coworkers. Nor do they allow
useless or unnecessary information to motivate them.

They consider how things relate to them, then make a decision and take action. They're good at blocking out superfluous information and external influences, such as what other people say or do.

> Those who have the power to let
> things go are able to spend their
> days in relative ease.

They aren't weighed down by regret, nor do they waste time worrying about things that have yet to happen. They don't torment themselves. They're good at letting go of things they can't control, things that are inevitable, things that are in the past.

> They know what they
> ought to let go of.

Doing so gives them clarity of mind and heart, enabling them to concentrate on what's important. By minimizing complications, they are free to live their best lives, in good health and comfort. There are many things in this world that we cannot control. Other people, the past, the future . . . let all those things go. Instead of allowing them to consume our mind and our energy, it's better to devote our efforts to what we can achieve in the moment.

There is a Zen expression, *hogejaku*, which means "Let go of everything." As that saying shows, a life in which you are able to let go is a Zen life.

Of course, at work or in relationships—as in everything in life—there will be things you can't let go of. How do you distinguish between what you ought to let go of and what you ought not to? I will address all of that in these pages.

I deeply hope that this book will help you learn how to let things go—and how to live your best life, in good health and comfort.

Gassho
SHUNMYO MASUNO

HOW TO LET THINGS GO

Part One

DON'T GET OVERLY INVOLVED.

*Be more detached in your
relationships.*

1

LET THINGS GO AND YOUR LIFE WILL IMPROVE.

An indispensable life skill

Now is the time
to decide what to let go of.

You might think that to "let things go" has negative connotations.

To give something up halfway through, to leave something unfinished, to ignore an injustice, to neglect to follow up . . . aren't these the kind of things that are associated with letting go? They all seem to imply a sense of irresponsibility.

There's definitely some truth to this. In the examples above, I'd have to admit that to "let things go" seems unfavorable.

But in this world there are many things you'd be better off letting go of. Especially nowadays, when we are constantly inundated with information and when social media has made our personal relationships round-the-clock affairs, it's impossible to respond to everything.

This is precisely why it is all the more crucial to learn how to let things go. Really, we ought to refer to it as a survival skill.

Now more than ever, it's imperative to be able to differentiate between what we ought to hold on to and what we ought to let go of, in order to live our lives to the fullest.

2

LEAVE PEOPLE ALONE.

*This ability is essential for
personal relationships.*

There is a fine line between being attentive and being meddlesome.

How do you react when someone is overcome with worry? People often do one of two things.

One option is to say something to try to cheer them up.

Another option is to say nothing, to do nothing, to leave them alone.

There is no right way to respond. I will merely say that often, the first option can be considered being meddlesome while the second might be seen as being attentive.

When someone is worrying about something, they often need some time to worry—alone. They are simply not in the mood for someone to tell them to do this or that, to encourage them to cheer up, or even to invite them out for a drink "to take their mind off things." Managing any response can be hard on them. It's often just more trouble.

Think about how you'd feel if you were in their situation, if you were the one worrying about something. Wouldn't you prefer to be left alone for a little while, until you've had a chance to calm down?

3

CHANGING OTHERS IS
IMPOSSIBLE.

*The only person you have control
over is yourself.*

First, *you* change.

"My husband never puts things back where they belong, leaving his socks wherever he likes—he doesn't lift a finger to clean up after himself. After all these years of marriage, he's incorrigible, no matter how many times I ask him!"

I sometimes hear this kind of thing from people who are married, though it's hard to tell whether they mean it as a significant concern or a real complaint.

Here is how I typically respond:

"I admire your perseverance, but you're never going to be able to change your partner. You'll be much more at ease if you just accept them the way they are."

Worrying over little things like this only makes your own life more difficult. In matters great and small, there are precious few instances when things go exactly the way you want them to. Put another way, it may be that the only time you get what you want is when it has to do with yourself.

It's time to let go of others who are beyond your control. Better to focus on how you can change in order to make things go smoothly for yourself. And when you change, there's always a chance that others' behavior may ease up and move things along as well.

4

———

IF PEOPLE KNOW ONLY
THE HALF OF YOU,
THAT'S JUST FINE.

*Actually, even thirty or
forty percent is enough.*

Better to have a
more practical perspective.

Lately, there seems to be a noticeable increase in people who desperately want others to know everything about them. One sign of this is their need to post every detail of their lives on social media.

Another version is people with social-media friends—the majority of whom they've never met—who relentlessly post and respond to one another about every last thing they're doing. It seems to me that this constant communication sends the message "Pay attention to me—here, now, everywhere—understand me!"

I don't mean to discourage such earnest feelings, but no one will ever understand everything about you. You will never completely know your friends, either.

Realistically, you can consider yourself lucky if you have a few friends with whom you share about half of what there is to know about one another. We should be grateful for even a thirty- or forty-percent connection. A close relationship with a vast number of people—and the desire for one in and of itself—is a delusion.

5

THEY MAY BE FAMILY,
BUT THEY ARE
DIFFERENT FROM YOU.

*Assuming they will understand you
is a foolish mistake.*

The important thing is to have respect for one another's lifestyles.

It is said that blood is thicker than water. It may very well be that the bonds you share with your blood relations are stronger than the ones you have with other people.

However, the saying doesn't mean simply that because you're related there is an automatic understanding between you and your family. Family members are still their own people, each with different personalities, tastes, values, and views, so perfect harmony is impossible. The more you strive for it, the less attainable it becomes.

The important thing to remember is that your family may be kin, but they are not the same as you. You must have mutual respect for each other's lifestyles. You must treat them with patience and acknowledge their opinions, not impose your own upon them.

The worst thing you can do is dismiss someone in your family out of hand when they act in a way that doesn't make sense to you. This tends to happen when you operate under the assumption that because you are family, you'll always understand each other. It's fine to offer advice—just don't forget that they are different from you.

6

WHEN YOU DON'T UNDERSTAND, LET IT GO.

The secret to a happy marriage

There will be times when you don't understand each other, and that's okay.

The rise in popularity of the phrase "middle-aged divorce" may lead one to think that as a couple's years together accrue, their connection does not necessarily deepen.

It stands to reason that even married couples don't understand each other perfectly. If you get each other half the time, things are likely going well.

Before entering into a relationship, each person likely spent twenty or thirty years living a completely separate life. Even when people are from the same area, or have similar family backgrounds or interests, it can be quite a challenge for couples to understand each other.

So what can we do to connect with each other even a little bit more? If you know what the other person likes or values, or what their hobbies are, you can try to take an interest in those things.

And while you're at it, don't worry too much about the parts of someone that you struggle to understand—just leave them be. The trick to avoiding a middle-aged divorce is not to understand everything about your partner, but instead to find just a few additional things that you can share more deeply with each other.

7

IT'S OKAY TO BE DETACHED AT THE OFFICE.

Take care not to get too involved.

Let workplace relationships stay in the workplace.

Work relationships can run deep.

Socializing at work can range from midyear and year-end get-togethers to company field days and trip retreats—gatherings where conversations over drinks tend to veer into more private spheres. . . .

Workplace friendships can be very rewarding. After all, there is a saying about "eating rice out of the same pot"—that doing so builds a sense of solidarity.

But your work relationships will go so much more smoothly if you take care to keep out of your colleagues' private lives.

You might even say that, now more than ever, the times demand we be detached. Too much involvement could potentially lead to being entangled in problems such as workplace bullying, harassment by a supervisor, or sexual harassment.

The cardinal rule is to have conversations about private topics only with those who choose to open up to you. Keep in mind that you shouldn't be the one to bring up others' personal lives—let them come to you.

8

DON'T ISOLATE YOURSELF.
BUT DON'T BE CLIQUEY,
EITHER.

*Most people are
neither enemies nor allies.*

The essence of
the ideal personal relationship

Fear of isolation motivates most of our personal relationships. It's why people tend to form cliques—they are in search of allies.

But when a clique flocks together, it tends to root out outsiders or enemies from within its midst, flushing them out and crushing them.

Fundamentally, though, most of our relationships are not with enemies or allies. There are times when we join forces with someone and times when we find ourselves on opposing sides. The ideal relationship has this fluid quality.

We ought to be especially mindful not to regard as our enemies those whose opinions or mindsets differ from ours. The moment you begin to consider someone your enemy, your own sense of equilibrium is thrown off. If your enemy were to succeed, you wouldn't feel happy for them—you'd be jealous and want to drag them down. Conversely, if your enemy were to fail, you might gloat and say, "Serves them right!" It would turn you into a small-minded person.

Try to think of them as a rival rather than an enemy. This shift in perspective tends to foster friendly competition rather than serious conflict and builds relationships that strive for mutual growth.

9

DON'T KEEP WATCH OVER
SOMEONE'S EVERY MOVE.

It repels rather than attracts.

People don't trust those who are always looking over their shoulder.

"If I do this, will he yell at me?"

"If I say this, will it annoy her?"

To avoid offending or upsetting others, it's important to take their feelings into consideration.

But your concern should be for their feelings, not for how your behavior could reflect poorly on you. When you keep watch over someone's every move, trying to adjust your behavior to theirs, it comes off as unnatural and arouses suspicion.

Everyone is different, and ought to be treated accordingly. In theory, if you interact with ten people, you might need to behave in ten different ways to get along with each of them.

But that would be exhausting. You might even lose sight of which version is your true self, and others may begin to doubt your sincerity. A consistent self—one that doesn't shift depending on whom you're with—is the key to establishing authentic, trusting relationships.

10

COMMIT TO OBSERVING,
NOT INTERVENING.

*This applies to interactions with
children as well as subordinates.*

Your intentions may be good, but better to have patience.

Some parents nag and criticize, perhaps because they don't approve of what their children do or how they behave. Likewise, some bosses needle their subordinates and issue directive after directive because they can't stand inefficiency and disorganization.

These tendencies may stem from parental love or a protective hope for someone's development and success, but they don't nurture a child's or subordinate's ability to think and act for themselves.

If you're like this, I understand how you feel. Your intentions may be good, but better to have patience. Try to observe silently, without making unsolicited remarks. This form of engagement will encourage your protégé's development.

Of course, if you feel like someone is headed for trouble, or if they are endangered, it's okay to intervene. Nudge them out of harm's way with some gentle advice. And if they seek further guidance, frame your response with, "If it were me, I'd do this . . ." Then go back to simply observing.

Unsolicited comments—whether you're the one making or receiving them—create stress. As elders or superiors, we should commit to observing, not intervening.

11

SAVOR YOUR ALONE TIME.

Don't associate with others just because you're lonely.

Follow in the footsteps of Saigyo.

I can't help but think that ever since we've entered this age of the smartphone, we have become averse to loneliness. Perhaps we have grown accustomed to constant contact with others, chatting with them as if they were by our sides. But it seems as though we can no longer bear to spend time on our own, or to have free time with nothing to do.

This is a shame. Time spent in solitude is absolutely crucial. You need time alone with your thoughts to consider where you've been and where you're going, to question your behavior, to examine events that have happened in the world and how they affect you. . . . The list goes on and on. And so long as you are surrounded by others, you cannot get that alone time.

Since ancient times, Japanese people have regarded a quiet life alone, surrounded by the abundance of nature, as the height of luxury. The famous monk and tanka poet Saigyo (1118–1190), who lived from the late Heian period to the early Kamakura period, embodied this lifestyle.

We ought to strive for the awareness and introspection that alone time provides. It is a luxury that fosters a better way of life.

12

YOU CANNOT DO WHAT YOU
CANNOT DO.

Learn how to say no.

Don't become a
Jack- or Jill-of-all-trades.

When your colleagues, whether junior or senior to you, are swamped with work, lend a hand—it's the nice thing to do. But not when you also have your hands full. Gauge how much work you have and what your deadlines are, and then decide whether it makes sense for you to help out.

It's good to have people who can assess these kinds of situations and say no, but there are always some coworkers who struggle with this. Sometimes they even sacrifice their own work to assist others with theirs.

This can become a real problem if colleagues come to think of you as someone who will never say no—no matter what they ask of you. And because some people are shameless, they will bury you under a mountain of work "favors" and treat you like a Jack- or Jill-of-all-trades.

If you are at risk of being in this position, you need to let go of your concern that people might dislike you if you say no. Moreover, if both the work you offered to do for others and your own work end up not getting done, then you may have caused more harm than good. That's why it's important to be able to clearly communicate what you can and cannot do.

13

ABIDE BY FATE.

*Doing so will make
your life run smoothly.*

A way of thinking—and a way of living—that will lighten your spirit

"Fate" or "destiny" are words often associated with personal relationships, but they also relate to the minutiae of our daily lives. By allowing fate to guide our actions, we can enable our lives to run smoothly.

If something doesn't go your way, you might say, "It wasn't in the stars." This could be not getting into a certain college, not getting a job at a particular company, a business deal falling through, a project being terminated, an invitation you had to decline because of a schedule conflict, a romantic prospect you never managed to get to know. . . .

Isn't it liberating to think of all of these as things that were just not meant to be? Doesn't that ease your mind?

Similarly, to resist fate by trying to force something to happen is not a good idea. Let's say a lucrative opportunity comes along, but you're already committed to something else—you ought to prioritize and honor your commitment by declining the new opportunity. It's a mistake to evaluate things based upon a simple calculation of profit and loss. Rather, you won't go wrong if you abide by fate. Indeed, your life will follow its natural course.

14

RESIST A REDUCTIVE ANALYSIS
OF PROFIT AND LOSS.

*Such calculations
will not serve you well.*

For those who tend to think in terms of binaries

Good or bad, loved or hated, fun or boring, easy or difficult, valued or unappreciated . . . when it comes to making a decision, people tend to think in terms of binaries.

Before you take on a project, especially at work, it's not uncommon to immediately weigh the costs and benefits: "Will this further my reputation?" "Will this help me in the long run?"

But when your decisions are based on profit and loss, things almost never go the way you imagined. You might think, "This project is too easy—they won't appreciate it even if I do a good job, so it's not worth bothering with it." But that doesn't mean there is zero chance it will lead to a bigger payoff.

On the other hand, if you say, "This looks like a worthwhile opportunity. If it goes well, I could get a raise and a promotion," there are still many things that could go wrong, even when you're personally invested in its success.

The important thing is to use your ingenuity to put your own spin on whatever chances come your way. That extra little something you provide will be valued and will help to ensure a positive outcome.

15

DON'T BE MANIPULATED BY
SOCIAL MEDIA.

*The internet is rife with
futile battles.*

Do not forget that social media is merely a tool.

Even presidents and other heads of state are now on social media, using it to weigh in on everything from trivial disputes to matters of national importance. It's hard not to see it as a terrific resource for the free exchange of information.

But if I may offer a piece of cautionary advice, it would be about the danger of being manipulated by social media. Without being able to see others' faces, people become less considerate, making it easy for arguments to escalate in intensity. To avoid these futile battles, the key is to maintain a certain distance and not to engage rashly.

And of course there is the problem of maliciously fabricated news proliferating amid all the information out there, with the potential for defamation and the fomenting of unrest throughout the world. It is important for those of us on social media to be able to discern what is fake. Social media is, after all, merely a medium for communication. We must make use of it wisely.

16

"BE HUMBLE,
BE HUMBLE,
BE HUMBLE."

Stop with all the bragging.

People are inadvertently condescending toward others.

It's remarkable how much people brag.

It's difficult to resist the temptation to show off. Perhaps it's the manifestation of our desire to be respected by those around us.

The more you brag, the more a kind of unearned confidence takes root in you. You begin to think you are superior, that you have certain talents or a gourmet palate or whatever it may be.

Social media has only encouraged this, and it now seems that more and more people, without even realizing it, are adopting a condescending attitude toward others.

This is unfortunate because people who act high-handed and arrogant tend to arouse anxiety in others.

So first, stop with all the bragging. Then check yourself regularly to make sure your words and actions haven't been condescending, and if you feel they might have been, remind yourself, "Be humble, be humble, be humble."

17

WIDEN THE SPHERE
OF GOOD CHEER.

*Cultivate your
complimenting skills.*

Quick and easy tips for
giving compliments

Nobody feels bad when they are praised. However disagreeable someone may be, it's possible to establish an unexpectedly good connection with them by offering some gracious words. This allows you to create a kind of sphere of good cheer.

But knowing just what to praise can be tricky. Choose something out of left field and it might distract and dampen the mood, whereas obvious flattery can seem inauthentic and disingenuous. Plus, it can be even more of a challenge to find something to praise about someone you don't know very well.

What's quick and easy is to offer a simple compliment about a person's appearance—their clothes or their belongings.

"That's a lovely tie. Where did you buy it?"

"I like that pattern on your suit. It looks especially nice in gray."

"Your shoes are always so shiny and polished. You know what they say, 'the shoes make the man.'"

And so on. Avoid apple-polishing. Find something they would appreciate, and then casually offer your praise. As long as it isn't off target, a well-chosen compliment always helps to foster relationships.

18

SET ASIDE YOUR FEELINGS.

That's the trick to getting along with your adversaries.

Another way is to close your eyes to someone's disagreeable qualities.

In your personal life, you would never choose to spend time with someone you hate. "We have nothing in common" is sufficient grounds to turn away from someone.

This is harder to do in your professional life. You cannot simply say, "I dislike them so I'm not going to have anything to do with them." If you're thinking to yourself, "I don't like this person, I wish I didn't have to work with them," it will show in your expression and demeanor, making it unlikely that your interactions will go smoothly.

So what should you do? You have no choice but to be practical. Maintain enough of a relationship to be able to work together, but don't go deeper.

There is something of a trick to getting along with your adversaries. When it comes to people you dislike, you tend to notice even more of their bad qualities, so do your best to tune them out. When they say or do something unpleasant, say to yourself, "Ah, here they go again," and try to leave it at that. Alternatively, change the subject or find an excuse to walk away—there are various options. The point is, if you can manage to set aside your feelings and stay unemotional in your professional relationships, you are likely to get along fine.

19

DO NOT PURSUE
THOSE WHO LEAVE.

Better just to say goodbye.

Leave encounters with others up to fate.

A coworker leaves the company.

A teammate whom you bonded with through grueling practices quits the team.

A regular drinking buddy gets transferred and moves away.

However it may happen, the loss of a friend is painful. Your attachment can be so strong that you feel like rushing after them.

But as the Zen saying goes, "Do not pursue those who leave." It's best just to say goodbye rather than to prolong the pain of separation. After all, when a relationship breaks off, it's simply the end of the bond that held you together in that particular way. Sometimes the connection can be restored, or it may turn into an on-again, off-again kind of relationship.

Just as important is the second part of the Zen saying: "Do not turn away those who come to you." The crucial thing is how and when you meet someone, what brings you together. Human connection cannot be manipulated— it's more like a natural twist of fate. So in that spirit, "Do not pursue those who leave nor turn away those who come to you."

20

LEAVE PAST GLORIES
IN THE PAST.

*Don't linger before moving on to
what awaits you next.*

How to know when to gracefully take your leave

On any uphill path, there comes a point when you know "here is where the ascent ends."

This applies equally to life and work.

Even when everything is going smoothly, an "up" cycle cannot last forever. At a certain point, things shift downward.

Especially at work, if you can't see when that certain point is—say, when you should retire—then your influence will only diminish and you risk clinging to past glories.

To avoid this, set goals for yourself. Once you've achieved them and attained whatever measure of success you sought, consider that a tipping point.

Let go of any lingering attachment to how much fight you still have in you—better to step aside and pursue a different challenge.

Remember that the ideal time to take your leave is when you're at your height. Then it's time to move on to a new stage.

21

BE WARY OF NEGATIVE PEOPLE.

*It can be dangerous even just to nod
in agreement with what they say.*

It's wise to keep as much distance as possible.

People often let their negative emotions go unchecked, affecting those around them.

They might cause alarm by raising their voice and ranting and raving.

Or they might make people uncomfortable by glaring or scowling.

Or they might wreak havoc by airing their complaints to anyone and everyone.

Or they might dampen everyone's enthusiasm with their pessimism.

When you come across such types, best to steer clear of them. Plenty of people find it tedious to engage with personalities like that and instead simply nod along at appropriate intervals. But not saying anything is akin to getting involved, so better not to. All you did was nod, but now they see you as an ally and you could get drawn in even further.

Learn to detect when someone is venting their negative emotions.

And then keep your distance from them, literally. Excusing yourself to go to the bathroom is just one way to make a quick escape.

Part Two

DON'T WORRY ABOUT
EVERY LITTLE THING.

*How to relinquish anxiety,
impatience, and anger*

22

IF YOU CAN'T BE CERTAIN
ABOUT IT, STOP WORRYING
ABOUT IT.

It's best not to live in fear.

Deal with the problems that are in front of you.

At the root of anxiety is the desire to know something that you're never going to know, no matter how much you think about it. A classic example is vague anxiety about the future.

The future may be predictable to a certain extent, but we can never really know what will come to pass. Things that are one hundred percent likely to happen do not occur, and things that are one hundred twenty percent unlikely do wind up happening. No matter how much data you collect, no matter how much time or effort you put into thinking about it, predicting the future is hit or miss.

Of course, if you have worries about something that's likely to happen, best to do what you can about it right now. But there's no point in worrying about what may or may not come to be. You're better off devoting your energy to what is right here in front of you. If you focus on what you can take care of now, there's always the chance that the future you were worried about will change.

It's useless to fret about the future when you can't know what will happen. All we can do is try our best to deal with problems when they actually occur.

23

BECOME SKILLED AT
FORGETTING.

*It will safeguard
your mental health.*

Are you accumulating mental garbage?

According to one theory, the ability to forget is an instinct for self-preservation. If we remembered every last unpleasant detail from our day-to-day lives, it would crush our spirits.

As the old saying goes, "Once on shore, we pray no more." In other words, once time passes, it's human nature to forget the unpleasantness of almost any experience.

But while it may be good to forget trivial things, it's not good to forget things that are simply inconvenient or that you ought to have learned from. Rather than completely erasing them from your mind, perhaps it's better to keep things in a sort of memory drawer that can be opened and closed when necessary.

If something happens that you would prefer to forget, you should allow yourself to fully experience the negative feelings associated with it. But then you can say "enough" and place them in the memory drawer, thereby setting aside whatever happened.

Things you'd prefer to forget can build up and become mental garbage, but if you relegate them to your memory drawer, they can serve as potential for growth—so long as you sort them properly.

24

BE MORE AT EASE.

Put some distance between yourself and others' expectations of you.

Quietly go about doing what you need to do.

When your boss says, "I'm counting on you," naturally you feel like you ought to work hard.

That's all fine and good. But when you start to feel pressure to meet others' expectations, it can be both physically and mentally draining. You no longer feel the freedom to pursue something in a way that feels natural to you.

When that happens, instead of meeting expectations, you become anxious and struggle to produce results. But you mustn't torment yourself, since your ability to please others wasn't necessarily guaranteed to begin with.

Be more at ease. Your boss's expectations of you were always just that—your boss's. They were never your own. And regardless of whatever those expectations may be, you should just quietly go about your work in the best way you know how.

If it happens that your work doesn't meet your boss's expectations, then fine—you can simply try to do better next time. In this sense, it's good to put some distance between yourself and others' expectations of you. The more space there is between you and those who ask something of you, the less you will feel burdened by their expectations.

25

TAKE OFF THE
"GOOD PERSON" MASK.

*Before you lose sight of
your true self*

The danger of keeping your mask on.

When you wear a mask, it's impossible to see what your face looks like.

An archnemesis might be scowling at you, but if they're wearing a smiling mask and speaking in a calm voice, you'll feel very different about them. You could say that masks are extremely convenient for concealing one's true nature.

Even though you may not literally wear a mask, it's still possible to assume a false demeanor to hide what you're really feeling. That's just another kind of mask.

Everyone wants to be thought of as a good person. That's precisely what leads many people to put on a mask. But it's no good to just leave it on because you run the risk of forgetting what your true self looks like.

It seems to me that more and more people assume false personas all the time, perhaps because they are increasingly interacting on social media rather than in real life. That can be dangerous. They are living their lives behind masks rather than living as themselves.

26

DO NOT MEASURE YOURSELF
AGAINST THE AVERAGE.

There is nothing more futile.

No matter how much you feel compelled to make comparisons . . .

It can be demoralizing to compare yourself to someone and find yourself lacking. On the other hand, it can cheer you up to feel like you're better than someone else. That's human nature.

Nobody wants to be ordinary, so it makes sense that being below average makes us feel anxious while being above average makes us feel secure.

Nevertheless, there is nothing more futile than comparing yourself to everyone else. Since there is no universal standard for assessing someone's value, it's impossible to determine anyone's relative merit by comparing them to others.

If you insist on making comparisons, measure your current self against yourself at your best. Doing so may offer motivation for growth and development.

If you find yourself lacking when measured against your best self, try harder. And if you find that you have surpassed your best self, then you can set a new personal goal and continue to try harder. That is a good cycle to set in motion.

27

WORRYING ABOUT EVERYONE
ELSE IS A LOSING PROPOSITION.

Don't be taken in by statistics.

There's no such thing as an average way to live.

To continue the previous chapter's discussion of the perils of comparing yourself to the average, it seems like every day the media reports on statistical data about our lives. Average annual income by age group or industry, average age to marry or buy a house, average savings at every age, average amount of money necessary to live comfortably in old age . . . apparently lots of people want to know what these averages are.

But that's all they are—statistics. They cannot serve as guidelines for how to live. You may as well say your life's goal is to be seen as above average. But what could be more pointless?

You're much more likely to lead an enjoyable and care-free life if you don't worry about everyone else and simply follow your own set of values. Better to say, "I'm going to live my life this way. I don't know whether this is typical. But that doesn't matter, because I don't want to be guided by averages." Besides, there's no such thing as an average life. One function of statistics is to influence people's views and consumer behavior. Don't let yourself be taken in by the allure of statistics.

28

APPRECIATE WHAT MAKES
EVERYONE DIFFERENT.

*Do so and you'll never be insecure
or arrogant.*

The way to respect each other's individuality

Did you learn to compare yourself with others from an early age?

It's understandable. All of us, for as long as we can remember, have been compared with those around us—on everything from test scores to how fast we could run.

I've said repeatedly that we should stop comparing ourselves with others, but some of us just can't help it.

If you find yourself resorting to making comparisons, try telling yourself, "It's not about who is better or worse—we're just different. And it's fascinating."

You'll find that you have qualities that others don't have, and vice versa. You'll notice interesting things about others. You'll realize that we all have distinctive personalities, and that it's important to make the most of them.

Once you get to that point, there's no need to rank yourself against others and, it follows, no need to feel insecure or arrogant. Learning to enjoy our differences can help us improve our relationships.

29

DON'T BE SURPRISED BY
BROKEN PROMISES.

Take them in stride.

Think of them with empathy rather than anger.

Betrayals tend to fall into two categories:

One takes the form of broken promises. For example, "What do you mean you haven't started yet? How many times did I remind you about the deadline?" Or "You said you would definitely make it to our next drinks date, and now you're canceling at the last minute?" In these instances, you believed that others would keep their promises, and they betrayed your trust.

The other form of betrayal is even more of a letdown—when our expectations are too high and the results fall short. We tend to feel more cheated by this kind of betrayal.

Regardless of how we feel about a betrayal, the problem is our own—we're the ones who have to deal with it. In the examples above, the ones who betrayed us might say something like, "I promised to do it, but I wasn't able to and it can't be helped" or "I'm sorry to disappoint you, but I just can't be there." More often than not, betrayal was not their intention.

It's better to think of these disappointments with compassion rather than frustration. Don't be surprised by broken promises. Learn to manage your expectations. You'll be less likely to lose your composure.

30

"WELL, THESE THINGS HAPPEN."

These simple words will make you feel better.

Unanticipated events make life more interesting.

All sorts of things occur in life. You could say that life is just a series of unforeseen events.

But after you experience something once, what was previously unexpected becomes part of your life.

In time, you will be unfazed by it: "Well, these things happen."

It's often said that people mellow with age. Perhaps that's the result of an accumulation of experiences and the ability to say, "These things happen."

Life can be like a play with no script. All the more reason to take pleasure in improvising your role, don't you think?

And so when the unexpected happens, just say to yourself, "These things happen." You'll see that these simple words will make you feel better.

31

DON'T CURATE YOURSELF.

*Obvious ruses are cheap
entertainment for people
you don't know.*

Facing up to your true self

In the world of social media, the idea of curating yourself is common. People tweak how they present themselves until there's no way to know who they really are. Even those who know one another in real life curate themselves as part of this online game.

The problem arises when the desire to make ourselves look good or have people think highly of us leads us to embellish our social media posts with untruths or resort to obvious deceptions with our online photos and videos.

As long as you curate yourself, you will never develop into the person you truly are. To put it another way, you can present yourself to others however you like, but that won't make you any different on the inside.

So let's stop devoting our energy to this kind of thing. When you lie to others so they won't laugh at you, they might just make fun of you for trying too hard. Better to focus your efforts inward. That may be the true meaning of curating yourself.

32

IF YOU'RE GOING TO JUDGE
YOURSELF, DO IT AGAINST
YOUR "YESTERDAY SELF."

*Change the subject of
your comparison.*

Stop judging yourself
from the outside.

While we're on the subject of curating, here's one more thing: when we decide which aspects of ourselves to showcase, we often do so based upon others' perspectives. Rather than asking, "How do I see myself?" we usually ask, "How am I seen by those around me?" And the answer to that determines our behavior.

If you post about something that others wish they had or could experience, you often get a barrage of likes. This may make you feel good, but it's pointless if you misrepresent the facts to make yourself look better. The gap with reality widens, and eventually you will be unable to maintain the ruse.

You are both no more and no less than yourself. You need only to see yourself as you are, and to present yourself as you are, no matter what other people's successes may be.

From this day forward, learn to evaluate yourself not based on how you think others perceive you but compared with your "yesterday self." Then you can take pleasure in the fact that today you're able to do something you weren't able to do yesterday. And I predict that, little by little, you will discover your true self.

33

IMMEDIATELY PUT THE THINGS
YOU'VE DONE FOR OTHERS
OUT OF MIND.

*Kindness is compromised when you
expect something in return.*

Expecting reciprocity will lead to disappointment.

I always say, "There's no honor in being patronizing when you help someone." And here's another adage worth taking to heart: "Etch kindness received into stone, let goodwill given flow like water."

When you have helped or cared for someone out of the kindness of your heart, you do not expect anything in return. If, however, you help with the assumption that there will be reciprocity, you create your own disappointment when it doesn't materialize.

I often hear things like, "I set him up with a great job but he has never said a word of thanks—how rude!" or "Whenever something goes wrong, she always comes crying to me, but if I have a problem, she pretends not to notice. Her selfishness is unbelievable." The best way to avoid these negative feelings is to immediately put the things you've done for others out of mind.

But do make sure to express gratitude when someone does something for you. Then pledge to yourself to assist them at some point—and act upon it. This is what I mean by cherishing your connections with others.

34

ALWAYS REFLECT
ON YOURSELF.

*You may realize that you, too,
were being selfish.*

Seek the path that will satisfy everyone involved.

When I look at how world leaders behave, it's hard not to despair that world peace is an impossible dream. Every country seems to insist on putting their own interests first.

Of course politicians work for the national good, so it's natural for them to prioritize their own country. But since the world is interdependent, it follows that if other countries aren't thriving, our country won't thrive, either. Seeking the path that will satisfy everyone involved is also the path to achieving peace.

This is the kind of thinking that Buddhism's Middle Way upholds. It works just as well on an individual level. Whereas the advantages and disadvantages of an agreement vary depending on one's perspective, the key is to look for a solution that is fair, with both sides making concessions and sacrifices.

Unfortunately, in recent years an extreme "me-first" attitude has become more prevalent. But before you criticize someone for selfishness, consider your own actions. By recognizing that you, too, may have been selfish, perhaps your relationships will improve.

35

GIVE THANKS TO THOSE
WHO SUPPORTED YOU.

*You can't achieve much
all by yourself.*

In every workplace, there are unsung heroes.

No matter your line of business, there are roles that are thought of as "one-person jobs." Take sales: there's one person who visits certain clients and lands a contract. The same goes for the preparation of various documents—whether it's a proposal or prospectus; a report; or the abstract, minutes, or presentation for a conference, most people believe they take only one person to create.

But in reality, there are hardly any tasks that can be completed by a single person. Most tasks require the cooperation of various people.

When you see things from this perspective, you recognize that you can't get much done all by yourself. Nevertheless, some people seem to take every opportunity to tout their own efforts: "That was my doing" or "We only got those results because of me." It's disgraceful.

You must not forget that for every supposedly solo job there are coworkers who offer their assistance and clients without whom there would be no project to work on. These people are the unsung heroes who support so many "one-person jobs." Make sure to express your thanks to them.

36

PAY NO MIND TO
MINOR DIFFERENCES.

*In the end, they're
nothing to worry about.*

Instead, pay attention to more pronounced differences.

Relationships between bosses and their subordinates tend not to go all that well when there is a small age difference between them. Beyond a sense of rivalry, other feelings may arise: the boss may not want to give in to someone they view as less experienced, or the subordinate may not want to take orders from someone only a few years older.

But when there are ten or twenty years between them, they're less likely to see each other as rivals. The boss can feel like they've still got what it takes, while the subordinate can offer the boss due respect.

The same can be said about job expertise, skills, and rank. Minor differences tend to elicit competitiveness. But if the difference is more pronounced, then the dynamic becomes less competitive.

However, it's the opposite that ought to be true. Shouldn't it be that minor differences are irrelevant? When things are quite similar, it's much of a muchness—nothing to worry about. Better to pay attention to major differences. If you set a goal to close the gap in rank or skills or expertise, you'll be able to focus on your own achievements and on improving yourself, little by little.

37

LEARN TO TURN DIFFICULT
EXPERIENCES INTO
AMUSING STORIES.

The key is to give them time.

We can get through most things
in life by learning
to laugh through them.

Hardship, pain, frustration, sadness, mistakes . . . some people have a way of telling amusing stories about things that normally would weigh heavily upon the listener. Sometimes doing so even helps the person telling the story to transform their unpleasant feelings about what happened and to lighten their spirit.

But it can be difficult to speak lightly of difficult experiences soon after they occur. And even if you manage to do so, those listening may not find it funny. You might alienate them by coming across as insensitive and seeming to make light of misfortune.

The key is to let enough time pass after what happened, to allow yourself to fully process how you feel about it— then things will mellow. The bitterness will mature into a milder form, like aged wine. As the rawness fades, it becomes easier to turn what happened into an amusing story.

No matter how unpleasant an experience may be, if you can talk about it with humor, you won't have to carry around your negative feelings. You can learn to laugh through most things in life.

38

STOP REGRETTING AND
START REFLECTING.

*How to make the most
of your mistakes*

Focus on the process rather than the results.

Often our regret about past mistakes is what sends our emotions in a negative direction.

"I shouldn't have done that."

"I wish I hadn't said that."

"If only I had made a different decision."

"I shouldn't have chosen to go this route."

We continue to feel regret about things that are over and done with, even when we know it's too late to undo them. It happens to everyone.

The important thing is to shift your mindset from regret to reflection.

"Oh, I did something wrong. But what exactly was wrong about it? Let me take another look at what happened."

See how you can view mistakes as an opportunity to learn and avoid future ones?

It's a way to remake how we carry the past with us.

39

DISPOSE OF THINGS
YOU DON'T USE.

*Getting rid of things
will lighten your spirit.*

These items are like
excess saturated fats.

During COVID-19 lockdowns, many people disposed of their unused items in one fell swoop.

This was a very good thing, what might be thought of as a silver lining to the pandemic.

When disposing of things you no longer use, though, you might worry about being wasteful. But don't. The more items you amass in your home that you don't use, the more heavily they weigh upon your spirit.

These items are like excess saturated fats in our food that bring about health problems.

Take unused clothing, for example. Create three categories: things you haven't worn in three years; things you've worn once or twice in recent years but that aren't your favorites; and things you don't get a chance to wear often but that you love. For the first two categories, regardless of how expensive these items were or if you think you might possibly wear them again, the best thing to do is to dispose of them. You won't only be getting rid of unnecessary clothing—you will also dramatically lighten your spirit.

40

RELINQUISH RATHER THAN
THROW AWAY.

*The clever way to dispose of items
while extending their life*

The subtle distinction between throwing away and relinquishing

Throwing things away is wasteful.

But really, there's not much difference between tossing something and simply stashing it away.

When you think about the life of an item, throwing it away and stashing it away have the same effect: you're not utilizing its potential.

Instead, consider relinquishing it.

Even after you've parted with something, you can give it new life by putting it into the hands of someone who needs it.

So it's great to extend the life of something by relinquishing it—whether you're able to sell it at a flea market or donate it or give it to a friend.

Doing so can alleviate your sense of guilt about throwing something away and can lighten your spirit by eliminating clutter in your home—you can have your cake and eat it, too.

Part Three

BE MEASURED
IN YOUR REACTIONS.

*Practices that won't
wear down your spirit*

41

DON'T TAKE EVERYTHING
AT FACE VALUE.

*Protections against
insensitive people*

When you wonder, "Just what was this person's intention?"

Why would someone say this?

What is the subtext behind what they said?

Often we cannot take people's words literally, and we are left trying to figure out their true intention.

The best indicators when trying to understand what someone means are their facial expressions and intonation. The way someone looks and sounds can convey their unspoken state of mind. We can glean important insight from these cues.

But there are plenty of people who just spout off whatever comes to mind, without any deeper meaning. And they do so without regard for whether their words might hurt someone's feelings. Most of them are simply insensitive.

There is no need to take what these people say at face value. Their rash, careless remarks are meaningless to begin with. Take to heart that it's no use to even react.

42

CHOOSE WHEN TO BLOCK OUT
INFORMATION.

An essential habit for inner calm

Don't leave your eyes and ears open all the time.

We see things that we would rather not see, that are better left unseen.

We hear things that we would rather not hear, that are better left unheard.

We know about events that we would rather not know about, that are better left unknown.

And then we cannot help but react to them.

These are hallmarks of an information society. It may seem like a good idea to collect information from a wide range of sources, but perhaps only up to a certain point.

It would be one thing if the information that came to our attention was all accurate, or if we needed it for our work or daily lives . . . but most of the time, that's not the case. All too often, its accuracy is dubious, it's of little importance to you, or it heightens your anxiety.

In light of this, is it really necessary to make an effort to collect every last bit of information beamed out into the world?

I recommend that you occasionally close your eyes and cover your ears to block out information. This will lead to surprising inner calm.

43

DON'T BINGE ON INFORMATION.

*Social distance yourself
from information, too.*

An essential mode of living
for today

Nowadays, we're bombarded with information at such rapid intensity that if you're not vigilant, before you know it you could find yourself buried under a pile of unnecessary news that has nothing to do with you.

During the spread of COVID-19, remember how everyone was talking about social distancing?

Perhaps it would be a good idea to put more distance between ourselves and information, too.

When you allow yourself to be inundated with information without regard to its usefulness or relevance, or when you binge on it, sooner or later your precious time and energy ends up wasted.

Decide for yourself what information you need and want.

That's a good way to establish just the right social distance from it.

44

DON'T WAVER SO EASILY.

*The cardinal rule when listening
to people's opinions*

Why are we so easily swayed by others?

There are plenty of people who will offer their unsolicited opinion about something you say or how you behave. Either they simply want to be nice or they like to pressure others to do things their way. Whatever the case may be, there's almost never a need for you to heed their advice. There just isn't enough time to take everyone's opinions seriously.

It's easy to get confused and to hesitate when making a decision.

"Alright then, maybe I should try what that guy recommends. But wait, she says to do the opposite. Huh? I didn't even know that was an option. . . . What should I do?"

To avoid this uncertainty, you must be clear about your own values before you listen to someone else's opinions. You need to establish what's important to you—the fixed objective that motivates you to take action.

Only then should you listen to those around you, thanking them and keeping their advice in reserve for the time being. Doing so will keep others from having too much influence over your decisions, and I think you'll be better able to draw on their advice.

45

ADMIT WHAT YOU DON'T
KNOW WITH DIGNITY.

*It's okay if people think you're
behind the times.*

If you want to know something, all you have to say is "Tell me about it."

When information is so abundant and accessible, people have a greater tendency to show off how much they know.

As a result, because social media is where information is disseminated, it can seem as if there's an endless stream of posts and messages where people brag about their knowledge and know-how.

The real problem, though, is for those of us on the receiving end. Whether in an online exchange or an everyday conversation, it's all fine and good when we're able to say, "Oh, yeah, sure, I know that." But when there's something we don't know, we feel oddly uncomfortable.

If someone reacts with something like, "What?! You don't know?" you might feel marginalized, as if you've been left behind or are the odd one out.

All we can do is try to take it in stride when, inevitably, there are things we don't know. Without feeling weird or awkward or self-conscious about it, try saying with dignity, "I didn't know that."

And if it's something you're curious about, you can express interest and find out more—and if not, just shrug it off. This is another instance when it's wise to social distance yourself from information.

46

"SLOW DOWN,
SLOW DOWN,
SLOW DOWN."

*A simple refrain
to quiet your mind*

Even monks get angry sometimes.

Everyone loses their temper at some point. Maybe your pride is hurt when you feel you've been insulted, or you're accused of something you were unaware of and it makes you want to shout, "Stop messing with me!"

But taking out your anger on someone else doesn't solve anything. And it's futile to step into the ring and fight with someone who has offended you.

Let me show you the best way I know to alleviate your anger in three seconds. Chant to yourself something along these lines, in a soothing tone:

"Gratitude, gratitude, gratitude."

"Slow down, slow down, slow down."

"Hold it, hold it, hold it."

"It's alright, it's alright, it's alright."

Almost any variation on these phrases will work.

I learned this from the late Koshu Itabashi, who was the abbot of a Soto Zen temple. Even monks get angry, but we have to know how to pause and not give in to our temper.

47

———

BE AWARE OF
WASTEFULNESS.

There are many things that
don't need to be done.

Streamline your work and tasks.

COVID-19 robbed us of the everyday life we took for granted.

But it also opened our eyes to so much that is unnecessary about modern life, like how much time we had been wasting on work and tasks that either don't need to be done or don't matter.

For instance, how did you find remote work?

"There were surprisingly few meetings and appointments I needed to attend."

"Part of the work I had done in person could be done remotely."

"I saved a lot of time by not having to commute."

Many of us came to similar realizations. We were able to sort the work that was important from the work that didn't matter.

What if we gradually gave up or reduced the frequency of our less important work and tasks? We would eliminate waste and would likely significantly increase the time we spend on what's important.

48

DON'T GET INVOLVED
IN THINGS THAT
DON'T CONCERN YOU.

Act in a more purposeful way.

Do you meddle in other people's business or make hasty commitments?

What do you consider important?

What do you think you're capable of?

Failure to keep in mind the answers to these two questions can lead you to get involved in things that don't concern you.

At work, you might set about doing something that doesn't need to be done immediately, without considering your priorities. You have your own projects that you should work on, but instead you offer to help with someone else's assignment. You hastily commit to something that is far beyond your ability.

Or in your personal relationships, you butt into matters that have nothing to do with you. You meddle in others' affairs or offer unsolicited advice.

This kind of behavior saps your time and energy.

Consider things that aren't important to you as unnecessary, and things that you aren't capable of as not worth your time.

Such practical thinking will enable you to act in a more purposeful way.

49

EXPRESS YOURSELF
JUDICIOUSLY.

That's the way of the wise.

Being a know-it-all
can be dangerous.

It is ill-advised to speak (or post) recklessly, repeating information that you heard someone speak about only briefly or that you saw on television or that was trending on social media.

You intervene in someone else's problems, brandishing unverified information and spouting off about how people should do this or that.

Or you launch into a personal theory about something you only partly understand.

It's best to refrain from saying and doing such things. Careless remarks are likely to confuse those around you. It's easy for rumors and gossip to spread, kindling a firestorm of disinformation.

Especially at work or with family, be careful not to speak up unless you know that your information is accurate or it's a subject you're well-versed in. Otherwise, you risk causing harm.

Words are important. Express yourself judiciously.

That's the way of the wise.

50

PAUSE FOR A MOMENT
BEFORE REPLYING.

*The perils of
responding too quickly*

This is how unpleasant email exchanges happen.

Emails and texts have become our primary means of communication. The convenience of contacting others whenever you want, at any time, in any place, is too great—there's no going back.

That's fine. Email and text to your heart's content. Just be careful not to respond too quickly.

If the message is pleasant, it's fine to reply quickly. But if you get bad news, pause for a moment. Because when you're in the grip of negative feelings such as disappointment, anger, or frustration, you risk responding carelessly. Sure, it's unpleasant to receive bad news. But when you send an unpleasant note in return, the situation can escalate.

Once you've replied, you can't take back what you've said. All the more reason to pause for a moment. Try to keep your negative feelings in check so they don't boil over. If you can do that, you can keep your cool and avoid saying something you might regret.

51

SLOW DOWN.

*Where are you going
in such a rush?*

Not everything is urgent.

Communication over smartphones, mainly among young people, just gets faster and faster. As an old man, I can't help but wonder, why not just call each other on the phone? But I guess it's more fun to send photos and videos than to just talk, and lately even seniors, too, seem to be doing this kind of thing.

A quick message is usually met with a quick response, and then you're locked into monitoring your smartphone at all times. This is all fine and good so long as the exchange is happy and carefree, but if the messages cause offense or anger or irritation, then you can't very well remain at peace.

I did a talk once with a psychiatrist, and one of the things he said was that while some people feel anxious when they are away from their smartphone, constantly having your smartphone in hand actually creates stress.

You don't need to be in such a hurry to respond. If the matter isn't urgent, it's okay to let it go for a few hours or even a few days. Try to remember to slow down.

52

DON'T ALLOW SADNESS
TO LINGER.

*The Zen teaching
"Be of one essence"*

Try not to wallow
in your emotions.

There is nothing sadder than the passing of a family member or close friend. Some people may linger in their sorrow and never really recover.

In such circumstances, consider this Zen saying:

"Be of one essence."

When we experience intense emotion—not only in times of sorrow or trying times, but also in happy times, inspiring times—we become one with those emotions. We experience life fully. And then in the next moment, our feelings shift and we must go on with a brand-new day.

That's the Zen way of life.

When you don't take the time to be of one essence, your emotions can remain unresolved and are left to linger with you. That's what it means to wallow in your sadness.

And that's why when you're sad, it's better to cry your eyes out without worrying what anyone else thinks. In due time, you will find the strength to pull yourself back up.

53

"WOW. I CAN BE SO SMALL-MINDED."

Recognize good things for what they are.

When jealousy rears its head, use this as a reminder.

Humans are jealous creatures. But what feelings are at the root of jealousy?

When we see a partner or someone we're fond of becoming friendly with someone else, we get jealous, don't we? We feel a strong urge to monopolize them, to keep them for ourselves.

Or when a rival has a big success, it's difficult to say "Congratulations!" with genuine pleasure, isn't it?

This stems from a superiority complex, from our desire to be number one.

And it's not limited to romantic relationships or the workplace—it extends to your family, your alma mater, your looks, your possessions, your knowledge, your athleticism, your popularity, and so on. We feel the same envy of those who enjoy a higher standing than we do.

But when these jealous feelings come over you, what if you said to yourself, "Wow. I can be so small-minded."

A bighearted person is able to acknowledge that something wonderful is genuinely wonderful. We should strive to be open-minded and generous.

Bigheartedness is a significant aspect of one's personal charm.

54

LIVE YOUR LIFE
INDEPENDENTLY AND
TO THE FULLEST.

*A way of living unaffected
by everyone else*

Just who is this
"everyone" anyway?

"But everyone has one!"

When you were a child, did you ever pester your parents like this when there was something you wanted?

I doubt many parents said, "Well, if everyone has one then I guess there's nothing to do but buy you one, too." More likely, they responded with something like, "Really? And just who is 'everyone'?"

Of course, both children and adults are well aware that there's nothing much behind this "everyone." And yet when we hear "That's what everyone says," we assume it must be what eighty or ninety percent of people think. Maybe that just illustrates how much we want to be like everyone else. But you cannot live your own life if you are constantly swayed by the crowd. Banish the meaningless "everyone" from your mind and strive to live your life independently.

55

TRY TO SEE THINGS FROM A
DIFFERENT PERSPECTIVE.

*The way things look changes
depending on your viewpoint.*

Are those your assumptions?

There's nothing more troublesome than preconceived notions. People cling to them fervently, convinced they are right, and nothing anyone says will change their minds.

Implicit in that righteousness is the attitude that one side is correct and any other viewpoint is incorrect.

Aside from principles that will remain true over tens, hundreds, and thousands of years, the things that people insist are right "because I said so" reflect a subjective value system. And so it is necessary to question our assumptions and how they influence what we believe to be right.

Ask yourself: "What if I looked at this from a different point of view? Am I sure that my perspective is correct?"

By questioning this, your visible landscape shifts. You allow yourself the space to consider opinions and ways of thinking that differ from your own. When we cast aside our assumptions, we can seek out the truth from a variety of perspectives.

56

RETHINK THE ADAGE
"HE WHO KNOWS LITTLE
OFTEN REPEATS IT."

*Fear a lack of ingenuity
more than failure.*

An anecdote about a Zen monk and a wealthy merchant

There is a story about the Soto Zen monk Honko Fugai.

While the monk was at his shabby temple in Osaka, a wealthy merchant came to him for guidance. As the merchant revealed the details of his struggles, the monk couldn't help but fix his attention on a horsefly buzzing around them.

In an attempt to get outside, the horsefly had crashed into the shoji paper screen door and fallen to the floor, apparently dead. But a short while later, it was up again and buzzing around the shoji screen until it crashed once more . . . and then proceeded to do this over and over.

Wherein the monk and the merchant had the following exchange:

"This poor horsefly," the monk said. "The shoji doors in our humble temple have holes all over, not to mention the other crevices here and there, and yet all it does is try to go through the same spot on the screen. It will surely die."

The merchant replied, "All you're doing is watching the horsefly, paying no attention to my problems. Do you find this horsefly so fascinating?"

"Oh, I was just marveling that we humans are the same. We can see things from only one perspective, and so our problems will always remain unresolved."

The merchant suddenly realized how aptly this applied to him.

57

TAKE TO HEART THE MAXIM
"TO EACH THEIR OWN."

*Personal values come in a thousand
shapes and forms.*

It's important to find common ground.

If you take a hundred people, every last one of them will differ in terms of their faces, body types, abilities, and personalities. We all vary from one to another. Our values, too.

And those values are not right or wrong, nor is there an order of merit to them. One's values deserve respect. Nevertheless, many people refuse to acknowledge others' values, and even insist that only their own are right.

What's worse is when people deny and criticize values that differ from theirs. Or when they try to impose their values on others. They may say things like, "You don't drink? You don't go to the racetrack or the casino? Do you even enjoy life?" The appropriate response, of course, is to ignore such things, or simply shrug them off.

Let people like that serve as a reminder not to deny or criticize the values of others. It's important to respect others' values, even if they conflict with your own, and to listen openly to what they have to say. While taking in their perspective, compare it to yours and try to find common ground.

58

DON'T EXPECT TOO MUCH.

Everything will go more smoothly.

Have the attitude that "if things go well, it's lucky."

There is something quite difficult about expectations—both having them of others and being subjected to others' expectations of you. Of course, having expectations of someone is also a way of hoping for their growth or success. There's nothing wrong with that. And being the subject of someone's expectations can inspire you to work harder to live up to their belief in you.

So I'm not telling you not to have expectations. It's expecting too much that's no good. The higher your expectations, the bigger your disappointment when they're not met. You may also be tempted to express your dissatisfaction: "I expected so much from you . . ."

And when you're subjected to someone else's expectations, their high hopes can put pressure on you, affecting your ability to perform.

Moderate expectations can have a positive impact on performance, but unrealistic ones can be a burden and be counterproductive.

It's not every day that things turn out the way we expect them to. You'll feel better if you have the attitude that "if things go well, it's lucky"—that way, it's hard to be disappointed if the results come up short, and you'll be doubly pleased if they come out better than you hoped.

59

IMMERSE YOURSELF IN THE
TASK AT HAND.

*By doing so, you shield yourself
from distractions.*

The important thing is to create an environment that enables you to focus.

When you immerse yourself fully in a task or project, other information gets shut out.

For example, even if the television is on, you don't see or hear it.

Even when people around you are talking, you're not listening to what they're saying.

If your smartphone is away from you, then you don't notice texts or missed calls.

I've seen this happen. Your attention is fully on the task at hand, and you are not distracted by irrelevant things.

If you do your best to reverse engineer this kind of environment—turn off the TV, sit by yourself, silence your phone—then you won't have to respond to each and every trivial thing that comes up.

Most things will work themselves out whether or not you are involved. It's okay to let some things go.

Wouldn't it be much more fulfilling to devote your complete attention to the task at hand?

60

YOUR PERSONAL
CIRCUMSTANCES ARE ALMOST
NEVER OTHER PEOPLE'S
CONCERN.

That's why excuses often fall flat.

The cardinal rule
when you make a mistake

When you're late or you're unable to meet a deadline or you forget what you were told to do, it's natural to make excuses.

This is motivated by a desire to help the other person understand your circumstances in order to explain why you made the mistake.

The person doing the explaining probably doesn't think of it as an excuse—they're simply making their situation clear—but to the person on the receiving end, that's exactly what it sounds like.

This is why the more elaborate your explanation, the more alienated the other person is likely to be—they may find you long-winded or inconsiderate or unconvincing, and they may wonder why they should care.

Unfortunately, as far as most people are concerned, others' personal circumstances are not their responsibility. It's no wonder they're unlikely to understand.

So rather than tediously explaining why something happened, especially when you're the one who made the mistake, it's better to just apologize and move on.

61

DON'T BE SWAYED BY TRENDS.

Just say, "No, thank you."

Beware of
getting caught up in fads.

The media—social media especially—uses clever tricks to start trends.

They make declarations like these: "This year the thing to do is rock the baggy look." "Blue is the 'it' color." "Here are the hottest design trends." They make it seem like anyone who doesn't follow the trends is hopelessly out of step.

In Japan, there were various public campaigns such as "Living your best life" or "A million-dollar savings plans for your retirement" or even the "Let's get cooking at home" push during COVID-19 lockdowns.

Each of these catchphrases is skillfully crafted to appeal to consumers' aspirations.

When you're constantly exposed to these trends and campaigns, before you know it, you're under their sway. And the result is the loss of your individuality. It's fine to take a moderate interest in trends, but when it comes to being sold a fad, just say, "No, thank you."

Part Four

DON'T WASTE YOUR ENERGY.

Ways to avoid making things more difficult for yourself

62

LOOK ON THE BRIGHT SIDE.

A practice to make life easier

Don't let your anxiety spin out.

Trying something you've never done before, going to an unfamiliar place, meeting someone for the first time . . . it's perfectly normal to feel anxious before doing something new.

But when you absolutely must deliver results or you have to apologize for making a mistake—who hasn't felt nervous under this kind of pressure? In such circumstances, it's easy to be pessimistic and to fantasize about all the things that could go wrong.

But consider this: Will spending lots of time worrying help? It will not. So try telling yourself this instead:

"There is no day without end. There is no rain without end. No matter how terrible, everything comes to an end."

Human beings are naturally pessimistic, so we cannot shift our attitude without conscious effort. Recite the words above like a mantra and take back the possibility of optimism. The more you're able to look on the bright side, the less anxious you'll feel and the better things will go.

63

DON'T GET STUCK
IN A NEVER-ENDING CYCLE.

The first thing to do is take action.

Do this to experience a breakthrough.

Everyone has felt that sense of panic when faced with something unexpected. Your mind goes blank and all you can do is repeat to yourself, "What should I do, what should I do, what should I do . . . ?"

As long as you're stuck in this loop, you may as well be at a standstill. So in such a situation, first let's enact a "force-quit."

It's like saying to yourself, "Stop! Start over!"

This will help you to break out of the negative spiral brought on by the what-should-I-do loop. Then, with your sense of calm restored, you'll be able to consider the following:

"What am I capable of right now?"

"What needs to be done right now?"

Once you take action, a solution will emerge.

64

BE CONFIDENT IN
YOUR OWN APPROACH.

*The secret to not wavering or
second-guessing*

It's possible to pay too much attention to what others have to say.

It's important to be open to the opinions and views of those around you. There are many advantages: you may get an idea that wouldn't have occurred to you otherwise, learn a helpful trick to get something done, or realize that you have even more options.

But it's also possible to be too open to the opinions of others.

"A. said this, which makes sense." "B. told me this. She's probably right." "C. recommended I do this. He has a point." All these opinions may confuse you and cause you to overthink things to the point that you're unable to decide what you should do.

To avoid this, you must first know your own mind.

This is what I think of as your own personal approach—the pivotal point from which you never waver. You are the protagonist in your own life.

If you don't commit to your own approach, then as you listen to other people's opinions, you might end up wondering, "Whose life is this anyway?"

65

DEDICATE YOURSELF
TO YOUR ROLE.

*It will be useful
to someone else, too.*

All work contributes to society.

In the course of your busy work life, you may have asked yourself, "Am I doing something that is useful? Am I contributing to society, even if only in a small way?"

During the pandemic, many people found it unsettling when more and more businesses had to shut down. They couldn't help but wonder, "Is my job necessary?"

But let me be clear: all work is useful and contributes in some way to society. It was COVID-19 that was unnecessary—not you or your job.

Something else that makes it difficult to recognize the importance of one's work is that many people work for large, complex organizations, and it can be hard to see exactly what impact you have in your specific position.

And yet, however small your role may be, the work cannot be completed without you. You just have to dedicate yourself to your role. Human beings are social creatures. We cannot live without our connection to society.

66

MAKE A SMALL CHANGE
EVERY DAY.

*A little trick that can
enrich your life*

If you feel like you're in a rut, try this.

You know you're stuck in the same old rut when life seems monotonous and every day feels like a repetition of the day before. It isn't necessarily a bad thing to pass your time peacefully and uneventfully, but when there's hardly any change from day to day, it can get you down. Life can begin to seem mundane and tedious.

But when you feel that way, it can be helpful to remind yourself that there's no yesterday that's the same as today. And there's no today that's the same as tomorrow.

If you think about it, it's not possible for every day to be exactly the same. The meals you have, your conversations with your family, the particulars of your job—there's always something even a little different from day to day. In our daily lives, we all have subtly new experiences, even though we may not be aware of it.

And if that isn't enough for you, I recommend that you consciously strive to do something different each day, no matter how insignificant. Soon enough this accumulation of minor changes will make today feel like today and tomorrow feel like tomorrow, and then you'll be better equipped to live every day to the fullest.

67

"RIGHT HERE,
RIGHT NOW, THIS YOU."

*Be fully present in the here, the
now, and yourself.*

An in-depth understanding of this simple truth

There is a *zengo*, or Zen saying, that encapsulates the need to live in the moment—to take action in the time and place where you find yourself.

"Right here, right now, this you."

We are only capable of living now, in this moment. The self that existed a second ago is gone, and there is no guarantee that your current self will still exist a second from now.

Likewise, you can only be in the place where you are right now, and only this you can take the action that is at hand.

That is to say, the core truth of life is that all we have is the now.

We must understand this simple truth on a deep level.

When we do, we can greatly reduce the amount of time we spend regretting the past, worrying about the future, and brooding, doubting, or agonizing.

There is action you can take now. Put all your energy into it.

This is what it means to be alive.

68

"CHANGE IS THE LAW OF LIFE.
AND THOSE WHO LOOK ONLY
TO THE PAST OR PRESENT ARE
CERTAIN TO MISS THE FUTURE."

*Both successes and failures are
already in the past.*

Work is truly a "living thing."

When it comes to your work, once a task is completed—whether successfully or unsuccessfully—it gets committed to the past.

Especially if your project is a success, it's common to think that however you approached it that one time is always the best way. The taste of victory is sweet, and you're unlikely to forget it.

Many people tend to hold tight to what has brought them glory—to believe that everything will go smoothly if they just go about something the same way they did it before.

But work is truly a "living thing." Everything—from the time, to the conditions, to the people involved—varies from one moment to the next. To simply follow the formula of your previous success does not ensure that all will go well.

You might even say that past successes can get in the way. It may be better to start over and look with fresh eyes at every new project in order to determine the best way forward.

John F. Kennedy said, "Change is the law of life. And those who look only to the past or present are certain to miss the future." I completely agree.

69

WORK IS FLUID AND DYNAMIC.

Be adaptable to changing circumstances.

Buddhist principles of work

Various tasks at work can appear similar, but there are always subtle differences. Buddhism teaches "All things in nature, everything that happens in this world, nothing stays the same," and this applies to work as well.

So you cannot have a blanket procedure for your work. You must approach each project in a way that suits its particulars.

When I design a landscape garden, I do a site analysis, which involves surveying the property from various perspectives, taking into consideration not only the sunlight conditions and soil quality but also the client (such as whether it is a corporate garden or a home garden), what time of day the garden will be in use, the state of mind of its users, and so on. I consider how to highlight the site's positive attributes and downplay its shortcomings.

I incorporate my detailed evaluation of the site into my design, in accordance with Zen philosophy, to create a space that reflects the site's virtues and the client's wishes. This differs greatly from the Western approach of leveling a site and then starting over from scratch. I believe that every kind of work requires a similar degree of customization.

70

DON'T PUSH THINGS OFF
TO TOMORROW.

*Do today the things
that need to be done.*

The teaching about "the negligent monk"

Here is an anecdote about the origin of Konnichian, the home of Urasenke Chado, one of the main schools of tea ceremony. More than three hundred and fifty years ago, Sen no Sotan, the grandson of Sen no Rikyu—who perfected the Way of Tea and founded the Urasenke School—bequeathed the tea room Fushinan, home of the present-day Omotesenke school, to his third son, Koshin Sosa. Sotan built a hermitage for his retirement behind the tea room and invited his Zen master, the monk Seigan Soi, to visit upon its completion. Sotan hoped Seigan would see the new tea room and give it a name.

The appointed time came and went, and Seigan did not appear. Reluctantly, Sotan went out to run an errand. When Seigan finally arrived and heard that Sotan had left him a message requesting that he please return the next day, he hastily scribbled the following reply on the paper *koshibari* covering the tea room's lower wall: "A negligent monk expects no tomorrow." That is to say, if an idle monk such as himself were told to come back tomorrow, one could not count on his timeliness. And that is how the tea room got its name, Konnichian, which means "Hut of This Day."

Seigan's message is interpreted to mean that you don't know what will happen tomorrow. You may or may not be here. So you must do today what needs to be done. We shouldn't rely on tomorrow for anything.

71

CULTIVATE YOUR STRENGTHS.

And leave your weaknesses to those
who excel at those tasks.

The ticket to personal growth

Everyone has strengths and weaknesses. And for whatever reason, many people work hard to overcome their weaknesses. The more conscientious the person, it seems, the more aware they are of their shortcomings.

Perhaps we try so hard because we assume that we must be good at everything in order to be seen as good in general.

There is nothing wrong with self-improvement, but what if you accepted your weaknesses as they are? When you aren't good at something, you may never excel at it, no matter how hard you try.

As I like to say, when it comes to your strengths, you can give one hundred percent and score a 100, but when it comes to your weaknesses, even when you give one hundred twenty percent you may score only an 80.

Your strengths tend to be things you like to do. And so you're motivated to do them, and you get good at them quickly. Your weaknesses, though, tend to be things you don't like to do. It's difficult to motivate yourself to do them, and you're slow to improve at them. So I encourage you to let go of your weaknesses.

72

DON'T FORCE THINGS—ON
YOURSELF OR ANYONE ELSE.

How to create a dream team

Each person should contribute what they're good at.

Companies thrive when their employees feel empowered. But the key is how well you perform as a team rather than how well you perform on your own.

Ideally, each person contributes one hundred and ten percent of their ability.

If there are ten people on your team, each skilled in a particular area, then everyone should be benefiting from ten kinds of strength.

This teamwork method has the potential to produce much greater results than individual workers who are directing their energies more broadly and not to their strengths, even if they have few weaknesses.

And the best thing about teamwork is that everyone can apply themselves to their strengths rather than having to do things they aren't good at.

With everyone on the team happy with what they're working on, you increase the chances of professional success and of the company also being happy with the results. Teamwork has such a positive effect!

73

LET GO OF
"BECAUSE HE'S A MAN"
OR
"BECAUSE SHE'S A WOMAN."

*Differences between genders
are simply differences
between individuals.*

Think of everyone
simply as their own person.

Several years ago, a number of Japanese medical schools were exposed for admissions misconduct. Administrators had been lowering female applicants' test scores on medical school entrance exams across the board.

The medical schools justified their actions by saying things like, "Women are more likely to drop out of the profession after marriage or childbirth" and "If there are fewer male doctors, emergency medicine and surgery departments could be at risk of being understaffed." All I can say is that it's unacceptable to discriminate against women and to penalize them on entrance exams.

I am involved in admissions at the university where I teach, and those who grade the entrance exams never see the name or sex of the applicant. So there is seldom parity in the number of men and women who are admitted, and the gender ratio varies from year to year. That's how it should go with entrance exams.

This doesn't apply only to universities—in the business world and beyond, it's no longer acceptable to discriminate on the basis of sex. One's sex has absolutely no bearing on ability.

Men and women differ the same way individuals differ. Those differences make us unique. Gender should not have anything to do with how we are evaluated. We should think of everyone simply as their own person.

74

ACADEMIC QUALIFICATIONS ≠
WORK QUALIFICATIONS.

*The important thing is to exercise
your talents.*

You cannot make it in the world with only your academic record.

One of my parishioners attended an academic-track junior high and high school but decided that he wanted to go out in the world and learn a trade. Rather than continue on to college, he got a job at a real estate company. At the age of thirty, he is now successful and independent.

Another young man who graduated from a technical high school and got a job with a leading residential home builder outperformed all the college graduates in the firm to become its president, and he has successfully expanded the company. "For me, education was not a factor," he likes to say. "I've always proved myself with the results I deliver."

People used to think that you had to graduate from an elite university and work at a blue-chip company to succeed in life, but that myth has been shattered. I think this may be a sign of society righting itself. It has never been the case that with just a strong academic record you could expect to coast through life.

You can get a college education at any time. Instead of relying on your schooling when you go out into the world, you can always make it on your own first and then enhance your résumé by continuing your education.

75

AVOID MAKING DECISIONS
AT NIGHT.

*Morning is the best time to make
important decisions.*

Nighttime fatigue and darkness affect your good judgment.

The more significant a decision is, the more important it is not to make it when your physical and mental energy are taxed.

When we're tired, we tend to be more pessimistic, and thus less likely to be able to see our options in a positive light.

People also tend to have less self-control at night, making it difficult to rein in your emotions and make clear-headed decisions.

Beware of answering important messages at times like this. Doing so can lead to bigger problems.

It's natural for mental and physical exhaustion and the dark of night to make you want to rest. Get a good night's sleep and replenish your energy.

Best to avoid making decisions when you're tired. Wait until the light of day when you're refreshed and ready to take action.

76

DON'T GIVE UP ON YOURSELF
OR GIVE YOURSELF
TOO MUCH CREDIT.

*Avoid labeling yourself as this or
that type of person.*

Don't wear colored glasses.

Preconceived notions cloud how we see others. Before you meet someone for the first time, you might do too much research on them—especially if you heard something negative about them—and what you find out can cement your impression of them.

This can lead you to misjudge them, making it difficult to get to know them.

As the zengo says, "Don't wear colored glasses." You must be careful not to judge others based on preconceived notions about them.

And "colored glasses" don't apply only to other people—you can manage to wear them when looking at yourself, too.

When we judge ourselves, we can be too lenient or too harsh. Either way, we cloud our view of who we really are.

Don't be quick to label yourself as this or that kind of person. Otherwise, you may give up on yourself or give yourself too much credit.

77

STEER CLEAR OF CALAMITY.

Be even more prudent when things are going well.

Therein lies the abyss.

The gold standard determines the value of money. Stacked up high, gleaming bars of gold literally dazzle the eyes, blinding us to anything else.

But what if a trap has been set right beside the gold? Ten to one, we fall into it.

Therein lies the abyss. Our suffering will be tremendous, in one form or another.

This is often the case with people in the business world who take bribes, commit fraud, or con others into money-making schemes that incur huge losses. Blinded by money, people lose their judgment.

Be especially vigilant when work is going well. Many temptations lie in wait, and because our guard may be down, we become more susceptible.

Whether bribes or scams, there are often traps hidden under promises of large sums of money. I urge you to be prudent and judicious.

78

REFRAIN FROM
INGRATIATING YOURSELF.

It will impede your success.

Fawning can trip up even the best salespeople.

In sales, if you can win over the key people in an industry or a company, you'll have a much better chance of securing big orders. With this in mind, many salespeople try to curry favor with senior executives. This can become excessive to the point of being unethical when it involves monetary gifts or lavish dinners.

If you see this kind of activity in your profession, you should refrain. Even if you were to successfully curry favor and win a contract, you would be in a compromised situation with your client. They have the leverage, leaving you, the seller, at their whim and making it impossible to maintain an equitable relationship.

And it goes without saying that there could be repercussions for any misconduct.

If your product is truly excellent, you won't need to bribe or flatter anyone to win them over.

Buyers and sellers should be on equal footing. Even the best salespeople need to be careful not to try too hard to ingratiate themselves.

79

WHITTLE DOWN YOUR
OPTIONS.

*Don't be swayed by
others' opinions.*

The rule for when it's time to make a decision

Sometimes it's helpful to gather opinions from as many people as possible.

Ideally, the more ideas you have, the wider your range of options.

But there's one major problem. Sometimes you get buried under a mountain of ideas, causing uncertainty and doubt to the point that you're unable to make any decision at all.

Things get particularly chaotic when you give equal weight to everyone's opinions. If you want to solicit ideas from outside, there should be a limit so you don't get paralyzed by indecision.

It's best to solicit ideas only at the very early stages of making a decision, and when it comes time to decide, only a select few people who are especially knowledgeable about the subject should be involved.

80

PROTECT YOURSELF AGAINST
BATTLE FATIGUE.

*You can also prevail by staying
above the fray.*

There are times when it's best to just step out of the ring.

In our hypercompetitive society, everyone and their brother seems locked in fierce battle—and not just corporate warriors. Even children study for exams with a kind of military discipline.

It's common to think, "I want to succeed in my job" or "I want to take the initiative and get ahead at work" or "I want to be highly regarded in my company and out in the world."

These goals are fine in and of themselves, but it's possible to get overly attached to winning the race. If you push yourself too hard, you risk burnout from mental and physical exhaustion.

It can be tough to keep up the fight, especially when your competitors are particularly strong or the goals you've set are difficult to achieve. The ancient Chinese classic *The Thirty-Six Stratagems* teaches that sometimes the best thing to do is to beat a retreat.

Another way this has been said is "He who fights and runs away lives to fight another day."

The wiser tactic may be to devote your fighting spirit to improving your abilities so you'll be on more equal footing with your competitors. There are times when it's important to duck out of the ring and replenish the energy you've expended in battle.

81

UP YOUR PLANNING GAME.

*Rules for taking on tasks
that people ask of you*

Avoid being vague about the amount of work you have or how long it will take.

When you ask someone for help with a project, it's important to be clear about not only the nature of the task but also the amount of work and time it requires.

It may be tempting to hedge about these things, but doing so can cause trouble for both parties.

For instance, you may say something like, "Oh, it's a simple job. I'm sure it will only take two hours." But if it ends up being trickier than expected, it could take more than twice as much time. The person you asked for help agreed to a two-hour commitment and now the project has become a major nuisance.

It also behooves the person who agrees to help to make it clear how much help they're willing to give. They might say, "I can work with you until three p.m., but then I have an appointment. You might want to ask someone else or even two others to help you, so that everything gets done."

To do a job well requires good planning.

Part Five

DON'T SEE EVERYTHING
AS BLACK OR WHITE.

*Hints for living
a comfortable life*

82

THERE IS NO SUCH THING IN
LIFE AS FORTUNE OR
MISFORTUNE.

Take everything as it comes.

The key to maintaining serenity, no matter what the day brings

Whatever is born will eventually die.

Whatever begins will eventually end.

These are universal truths.

Whatever problems may arise, no matter how much we struggle, there is nothing that comes to be that does not cease being and nothing begun that does not come to an end.

Likewise, nothing—good or bad—lasts forever.

If you can keep this basic truth of impermanence in the back of your mind at all times, then you will be less susceptible to the heights of joy when you succeed and the depths of despair when you fail. You will find stability in your spirit and in your life.

There is no such thing in life as fortune and misfortune. Whatever happens, you must take things as they come. Then you will always maintain serenity.

If something happens that sets your heart aflutter, whisper these words to yourself:

"Nothing remains the same, nothing remains the same, the world is always changing, everything eventually comes to an end."

83

THINGS ARE NOT INHERENTLY
GOOD OR BAD.

*Everything depends on
your perspective.*

Enjoy every day—
whatever it may bring.

In Zen we do not see things as being black or white.

So we do not discern inherent good or bad in what happens.

The zengo "Think neither good nor evil" teaches us not to conceive of things in terms of good or bad, and to avoid a binary perspective on life.

Rather, we're encouraged to think like this: "My experience is unique to this moment. There is nothing innately good or bad about it. Anything can be positive, depending on what I make of it."

Even when life is difficult or painful or sad, you can often look back on an experience and see the value of it.

Do not resist what happens.

All of our experiences provide the opportunity for growth.

Another zengo is "Enjoy every day."

If you live by this, you bring within reach the dream of every day being enjoyable.

84

ALL OF YOUR CHOICES
ARE THE RIGHT ONES.

*What matters is for you
to make the most of them.*

What you make out of your choices is more important than the choices themselves.

Life is a series of things you'll never know unless you try. Each time you might think, "Should I do this? Or maybe I should do that? I don't know which to choose!" But no matter how much you deliberate, it makes almost no difference.

Because there is no single right answer.

In *Alice's Adventures in Wonderland*, the Cheshire Cat gives Alice advice that is often misquoted as "If you don't know where you are going, any road will get you there."

Which is to say that there's no point worrying what is the right choice. If you'll eventually get to where you need to be no matter which option you choose, then all that matters is that you do your best with the choice you've made.

Once you let go of your indecisiveness, you will feel so much more at ease and your doubts will fade away. All that will be left to think about is how best to move forward with what you've decided to do. The results will follow.

85

BLOCK OUT
THE VOICES OF OTHERS.

*Pay no attention to their scorn or
their second-guessing.*

Ways to guard against those who criticize after the fact

In professional sports, it's the coach's or manager's responsibility to call the shots. Over the course of a game, they must simultaneously watch the other team's moves and make a series of decisions for their own team.

The challenge is that there are several ways to go about this, but they can choose only one. If their way doesn't work out, then they'll be filled with regret and conclude that they should have done something else. Even if they had, though, there's no guarantee that things would have turned out better. But too often we get caught up in the illusion of certainty that an alternative approach would have been the right one.

And then there are the commentators and fans who come down on the coach, saying this or that was the wrong call. But they're just Monday-morning quarterbacking— they criticize after the fact, with the benefit of hindsight. I can only imagine the strain of it all!

However, there's no need to worry about what everyone else says. As the well-known manager of a Japanese professional baseball team often asserts, "It was the best strategy for that situation."

It's the same in life. You call the shots in your own life, so even if things don't work out the way you hoped, there's no need to think of it as a defeat. Now that you have the benefit of hindsight, you just need to put what you learned to use for the next time. Think of all your decisions as being the best strategy you had at the time.

86

REGRET IS
NOTHING MORE THAN A
DELUSION.

*Anxiety about the future
is another delusion.*

Just forget about it and let it go!

Does regret or worry about the past gnaw at you?

Or maybe you tend to fret and obsess about the future?

Both are pointless and unproductive.

If worrying made the past disappear or dispelled your anxiety about the future, then perhaps it would be worth your time—but it does neither of those things.

Regret about the past and anxiety about the future are nothing more than delusions. It's absurd to let them burden you to the point that they get in the way of your ability to function.

Zen teaches us "Delude not thyself."

All we can do is concentrate on what demands our attention right now in order to turn our failures into opportunities for growth and to prevent our fears from becoming reality. When we immerse ourselves in the present, we leave no room for regret or anxiety to trouble our minds. Better to take action and drive away those useless delusions.

87

A FAILURE IS
LITTLE MORE THAN A STUMBLE.

*Get back on your feet
and redeem yourself.*

People who get a lot done also experience a lot of failures.

There's no such thing as someone who never fails. Or rather, the people who get a lot done also fail a lot. Failure is a given on your path to success, so it's nothing to get depressed about.

Long ago, in samurai culture, failure often meant you would be ordered to slit your own belly. But nowadays, while you still need to take responsibility for a mistake, at worst you may receive a pay cut or a demotion or a dismissal. It won't cost you your life. Think of failure as little more than a stumble.

Whatever the repercussions of your failure may be, you should be prepared to start over from square one. Once you've determined exactly where you went wrong, you can get back on your feet and into the game to redeem yourself.

Human beings are born into this world with just themselves. No matter how much is lost to failure, you can always go back to where you started. And from that point, there is limitless potential. The odds are never better than when you have nothing to lose.

Once you've suffered a setback, the best way to bounce back is to go all in on your next move.

88

SLOW AND STEADY
WINS THE RACE.

*Being too eager for success
can have the opposite effect.*

The perils of the shortcut

A journey of a thousand miles begins with a single step.

Rome wasn't built in a day.

Many a little makes a mickle.

Learn by watching an anthill.

Each of these maxims expresses that you can accomplish even the most monumental of undertakings by steadily and diligently working toward your goal.

It is also true that you cannot succeed without time and effort.

In our competitive economy, there's great emphasis on finding shortcuts in the name of streamlining and efficiency. That's fine if they work, but problems often arise with shortcuts, and what was supposed to be faster ends up taking even longer.

If you find yourself too eager for success, remind yourself that slow and steady wins the race.

89

HOIST UP YOUR DREAMS
RATHER THAN
HOLDING THEM CLOSE.

*The trick to successful
goal-setting*

The important thing is to always keep an eye on your footing.

It's important to have dreams and goals.

How big or small one's dreams may be varies from person to person. But there is one thing that I think should hold true for anyone: when you're working toward what feels like a big dream or goal, it's better to hoist it high rather than hold it close.

Because if your dream or goal is very ambitious, you can buckle under the weight of it and find it difficult to make progress toward it, and then you start to feel defeated by it.

But what if you hoisted it up high and set it out in the distance?

Then it can serve as a guidepost, making you lighter and faster on your feet, and better able to advance toward it.

But even when you've set your sights on your goal in the distance, it's important to keep a close eye on your footing, to be able to take the next best step with confidence and ease.

90

TAKE A BREAK, ESPECIALLY
WHEN YOU'RE BUSY.

*Even if only to allow
your mind to drift*

People who are good at taking breaks tend to perform at a high level.

Some people are so conscientious that they feel guilty taking time off. Think about those who go to work even when they're feeling under the weather. In Japan, in the initial months of COVID-19, we had to be urged to stay home if we felt the slightest bit unwell. Otherwise, many of us would have shown up for work anyway, and our conscientiousness would have given us a real reason to feel guilty.

There is an important lesson here about our relationship to work.

When you have reached a certain point, take a little break and look back on what you've just accomplished.

This can be restorative, of course, but it can also be productive. I like to refer to it as the unexpected advantage of the temporary lull.

You don't even have to take a day off. Just give yourself a few minutes in between tasks to stare out at the scenery or go up to the roof and look up at the sky or down at the world below—that alone is sufficient. Put this into practice, especially when you're busy. You'll reap the rewards of a well-deserved break.

91

NOBODY IS "NORMAL."

*Let "So many men, so many minds"
guide your social interactions.*

Mastering the art of communication through empathy

For some reason, we tend to assume that our own perspective on the world is "normal." When others see the world differently, we dismiss them as abnormal.

The saying "So many men, so many minds" makes it clear that there is no such thing as "normal." So let me say it again: nobody thinks exactly the same way you do.

With this in mind, the next time you have a conversation with someone who thinks differently than you, take care not to dismiss them. Listen to what they have to say, looking for something you think you can relate to, and then respond along the lines of, "I feel similarly about this point you made, but my opinion differs a bit in this way . . ."

Communication improves when you start off with empathy.

Remember that difference is natural, and that no one is the same as you.

92

DO NOT LOOK DOWN ON
OTHERS, EVEN WHEN YOU'RE
VICTORIOUS.

*Retaliation is
just around the corner.*

The perils of breeding resentment

Competition for wealth and resources has persisted on a geopolitical scale ever since the Age of Discovery, when Europeans began colonizing Asia, South America, and Africa.

In the corporate world, conquest takes the form of mergers and acquisitions. And on an individual level, it takes the form of harassment, intimidation, and bullying.

Whatever the circumstances, it's the way of the world that when one side crushes the other, you can bet that retribution will be severe. Even if we concede, for the sake of argument, that conflict is inevitable, it's humiliating when the victor imposes its culture and values on the loser.

Look at it from the perspective of the loser. To be stripped of your cherished culture and values would breed resentment, wouldn't it?

Subjugation fuels a desire for retaliation. I hope you've learned from this chapter what not to do. The next chapter addresses what you ought to do.

93

EXTINGUISH THE
SPARK OF CONFLICT.

How to win rivals over to your side

Learn from a renowned executive's triumph.

In the corporate world, the primary objective of business partnerships or mergers and acquisitions is to shore up each partner's weaknesses and to collectively boost their strengths and assets—by two or three or even fifty percent more than what they were before.

But when hierarchies come into play, things get complicated. The company that was acquired is often expected to surrender to the culture of the company that acquired it.

This does not serve either side well. Because everyone now works for the same company, it behooves them to integrate the best features of both sides and to respect each other's corporate cultures.

Kazuo Inamori, the founder of the electronics company Kyocera, oversaw numerous mergers and acquisitions, almost all of which were with companies that sought to be rescued from the brink of bankruptcy. Kyocera engaged in open and frank conversations with the employees of the companies they acquired, fostering connection and a sense of shared purpose.

It is crucial not to view your rivals with hostility, but rather to pursue ways to bring them over to your side.

94

YOU WON'T WIN ANYONE OVER
JUST WITH LOGIC.

*Brandishing your line of reasoning
isn't going to work.*

In some scenarios, a logical argument will get you nowhere.

There are times when pointing out the logical integrity of your position only makes the person you're talking to uncomfortable.

Has this ever happened to you? Someone flaunts their logic—"Well, you make a good point, but . . ."—and it really puts you off, right?

Why is that?

Because while a logical argument may make sense in theory, it often doesn't hold up in the messy complexity of the real world.

So it's best to stop brandishing logic like it's a secret weapon. It will often be rejected or disproved.

"I can see how this may be difficult to relate to, but . . ." is one tactic to move the conversation forward while you demonstrate an understanding of the other person's perspective. This makes it easier for them to express how they really feel, so that you can then seek a path toward resolution.

95

BE WILLING TO CEDE
SOME GROUND.

How expert debaters do it

A total breakdown
is the worst outcome.

In a debate, each person argues a certain position. This can lead to a clash of logic versus logic.

But as I said in the previous chapter, a logical argument can be unproductive. Both sides are likely to dig their heels in, unwilling to yield an inch, and then talks break down as the time runs out.

There are situations in which it's necessary to hold fast to your position, but more often a compromise can be brokered.

The purpose of any debate or discussion is to allow everyone to argue their point in order to reach a compromise or resolution. So there's no point in letting things break down.

Here's how to give an inch:

"I'll concede that point. But since that was a nonnegotiable item, I ask for your consideration. Can we find common ground somewhere?"

You get your point across while the other side saves face. It can be tricky, but this is a way to deftly settle a debate.

96

"ALL THINGS COME FROM
NOTHINGNESS."

*You can't take money with you—
not even a cent.*

If you're going to earn money, do it for the benefit of others to use later.

It seems the more money you make, the more you want. It's the same for everyone, and not just when it comes to money—it applies to all worldly desires. There are simply no bounds. Many people believe that if they make a lot of money, they'll get everything they want. Who could be happier than someone who possesses all that they desire?

But doesn't it seem futile to make all that money just for yourself?

Because no matter how much money you earn in your lifetime, you cannot take it with you. There is a zengo that expresses this: "All things come from nothingness." It means that we are born with nothing but our selves, and we die with nothing but our selves.

What you earn should be for the benefit of future generations. This outlook offers a new formula for a meaningful life: happiness = creating joy for the people around you. If there's still plenty of money when you die, you can designate in your will where to donate it so it can benefit someone else. And with this you will be free of the futility of having more money than you know what to do with.

97

SEEK YOUR OWN PERSONAL
MISSION FROM WITHIN.

*Then strive to fulfill it
with your all.*

A necessity for each of the seasons of your life

We are all born into this world with our own preordained mission.

You might think of it as your role to play in this life.

Do you know what your mission is?

You may well be thinking, "I have no idea."

But it's okay not to know.

I believe it's more important to go through life asking yourself the question "What is my mission?" than to know exactly what it is.

As you question yourself, you will begin to recognize the role you play throughout the seasons of your life, and then work as hard as you can to fulfill it.

The thing you work hardest at—what enables you to forget yourself—is the mission for which you are destined.

98

LIVE FREELY AND EASILY.

Be soft and humble, and thus,
true to yourself.

The Zen teaching of "softheartedness"

We all want to live our lives being true to ourselves. There are two points to remember.

The first one is to have what in Zen we call "softheartedness." This means, in a sense, that your mind's form is unfixed, like a cloud. It means you can respond to people and circumstances freely and easily, without the thought that things "should be this way" or "mustn't be that way."

It is in this freedom that your true self shines through.

The second point is humility. By this I mean the importance of using your abilities and talents to contribute to society.

When you force yourself to do what you're not capable of or something you're not good at, others may think you don't know your place. It can seem arrogant, and it's not true to yourself.

When you practice your talents with a humble heart, your true identity shines through.

Softheartedness and humility enable you to let go of the impossible with grace. Use these qualities to help you lead a life that is true to yourself.

99

DO YOUR BEST.

And leave the rest.

The quintessence of the phrase "How to let things go"

Whatever it is you're working on, go all out with it.

Just pour all your energy into it. Keep a clear mind and don't worry about whether you'll get a good result or what other people will think.

Just do your best.

Do all that you can, whatever is possible. What happens afterward is not your concern. Let it go.

Then you can just leave the rest up to fate.

All you can do is what you're capable of, and it's not up to you to determine what the outcome will be. Once you've done your best, there's nothing more to worry about.

There's something refreshing about doing your best and leaving the rest. Stop worrying about the outcome or your reputation. It will only disturb your concentration and cloud your mind.

THE ART OF SIMPLE LIVING

**100 Daily Practices from a Zen Buddhist Monk
for a Lifetime of Calm and Joy**

In clear, practical lessons—one a day for one hundred days—Buddhist monk Shunmyo Masuno draws on centuries of wisdom to teach you to Zen your life. With each practice, you will learn to find happiness not by seeking out extraordinary experiences but by making small changes to your life.

DON'T WORRY

48 Lessons on Relieving Anxiety from a Zen Buddhist Monk

Think of a time when you were worried about something, but then you realized how insignificant it was. Isn't it amazing how much lighter you felt? The key is to focus only on the here and now, thereby freeing yourself from unnecessary anxiety. By following this book's forty-eight simple lessons, you'll enjoy a calmer, more relaxed, more positive version of yourself.

life